Blue Violet: Haint Spaces

poems by

Samar Jade

Finishing Line Press
Georgetown, Kentucky

Blue Violet: Haint Spaces

Copyright © 2023 by Samar Jade
ISBN 979-8-89990-284-0 First Edition
All rights reserved under International and Pan-American Copyright Conventions. No part of this book may be reproduced in any manner whatsoever without written permission from the publisher, except in the case of brief quotations embodied in critical articles and reviews.

ACKNOWLEDGMENTS

My sweet children, Samuel and Silas; David, my adoring and ever supportive partner; the Vulture Cauldron that keeps me grounded in my truth; Sean Corbin, my first poetry instructor; Claudia Love Mair, my spiritual and creative writing mama; the Levee Collective; Bloodroot Ink; my ancestors who speak in my bones; Lexington Writers Room; the Ensoulment Community; Rua Mae; John Orduña; my TMT connections (aaaaalll of you); my siblings; Christine Yu and the endless depth of love that radiates through her legacy; every student I met while teaching: your creative authenticity ignited my boldness; Joy KMT; Cole of Rosie Cole Reads; everyone at Finishing Line Press; H.E.; Jay McCoy, Elizabeth Beck, and Katerina Stoykova; Ida Mae from beyond the veil; and anyone who ever showed me kindness and care: you were integral in my healing.

Publisher: Leah Huete de Maines
Editor: Christen Kincaid
Cover Art: Samar Jade
Author Photo: Ayna Lorenzo, Mothwing Photography
Cover Design: Elizabeth Maines McCleavy

Order online: www.finishinglinepress.com
also available on amazon.com

Author inquiries and mail orders:
Finishing Line Press
PO Box 1626
Georgetown, Kentucky 40324
USA

Contents

Prelude—"Do you get your period during a genocide?" xi

I.
Where I'm from 1
Abandonment 2
Cigarette 3
Rolanda Carries Full-Term 5
    First Trimester
    Second Trimester
    Third Trimester
    Birth
    Home
Untitled (for now) 7
To (M)other 8
Past Self 9

II.
blue 10
Destablized 12
Generated Inheritance 13
Mo(u)rning Dove 14
Athame 15
Trio 16
    Hold
    Shadow Holder
    Why do we hold onto the body?
Losing Guilt 18
Lump in my throat 19

III.
Duet: The breath I couldn't catch 20
weeds 21
Crushed 22
The door 23
Muntu 24
Blood of the Land 25
Black Femme 26
Affirmations to the Black Woman 27
Black Kiing 28
I am 29

IV.

When She reads 30
unto themselves 31
La petite mort de chocolat 32
An offered benefit of his friendship 33
Culmination 34
Compulsory Heterosexuality 35
Performance 36
Shores 37
sacral ache 38
Love Letter to a little Non-Girl 39

V.

1/5/2023 9:41 PM EST 40
Ship(wrecked) 41
wound 42
Named yourself Witch 43
Divine 44
marked 45
Why didn't they tell us? 46
Heretic 47
The Caul 48
care 49
In Remembrance 50

VI.

The Fool 51
Soul Met Body Met Soul 52
attachment 53
sensing 54
Einalia 55
Holy 56
soiled 58
Venus in Leo 59
Strawberry Moon 60
Unwrite 61
Silas 62
Samuel 63
altar 64

Postlude—"Our Breath is Revolutionary" 65
Encore: ungendering 67

Dedicated to little non-girl

Do you get your period while enduring a genocide?

Does the body take a pause?
Does it realize there may be no point
in
running through that cycle
when you cannot remember your last meal?
Or, that the ringing in your ears
is a perpetual scream
that
the night is not the terror
or that a maxi pad has become a luxury
when your body's driving force is to survive?

Does it tuck away its dreams for the living with the ever-rising number of the dead?

—To every femme bodied human alive in and around me that has suffered the ever consuming hunger of the oppressor

I.

Where I'm from

Where I'm from,
I cannot return.
That portal between my mother
and the soft deep is closed.

The memories twist round appendages,
piercing skin
like briar patches.
Each thorn, an epithet, a beating,
a strangling.

Cutting them away is pointless.
The tangled mess of branches
grow back from new places.
I forgot masked scars tread
the journey I've taken to
go back.

All lead me to some dusted crossroad.

Where I am from,
the love is all dried up
like a rusted bathtub knob
that sighs
in place of the water
you were in search of.

abandonment

I do not remember when it began
abandonment of self
The rage running white hot within my mother's eyes
The age of body, doubling in capacity, heaving in v-necks

"Oh my god! You need a bra!"
I can only remember how cold my body turned
knowing another aspect of me was yet utterly intolerable to her

Nine, maybe ten
I caught my first blood in homeroom
a wide patch of deepened red embarrassment
unfurled itself in the seat of my pants
Reluctantly, my mother picked me up from school
seething with anger veiled in smiles to the nurse
my needs rose above her expectations

"You're a woman now!"
she bit at me with bile
seeping through clenched teeth

"You'll have to start acting like a woman now, instead of little bitch."
Except, no matter how hard I tried
I could not find the place where a woman lived

My growing body betrayed me as the men turned wolves
and eyes consumed me
tore at my childhood

No, I do not remember when I learned
abandonment was the safest place
for me
safer
than the arms of my mother

Cigarette

He said he used to be a smoker
but, quit.
When I asked him why,
looking into the steel gray of
his Gemini Eyes
he said one day
he couldn't breathe
so
he stopped.
Just like that.

It reminded me of the moment I became aware
of the dangers of cigarettes.
I was eight in the 90's.
The acronym D.A.R.E
alive in my mind.
I was eight
sitting in the from seat of
a rusty Buick
Mama said
"Give me one of my cigarettes"
And,
I said,
"No, I don't want you to die!"

Backside of her hand met the left side of my face
"Don't tell me no and give me my goddamned cigarette!"

Hot tears stinging the skin
Skin opened by the rings that decorate hands that light Menthol
She takes a deep drag
The smoke fills her eyes with soft dissociation

The following night,
I met those same eyes
now wild
pupils widened.

And,
As I struggled to breathe,
the same ring studded hand now wrapped around my neck,
eight years too young,
She demanded I give her back
the "goddamned cigarettes"

I don't know what made her finally let go
But she walked out into the night
screen door wheezing behind her

I almost forgot why I told him the story
That's right.
I couldn't breathe
when he asked me
if I had ever smoked
a cigarette.

Rolanda Carries Full Term, 1985

First Trimester
It's crazy.
I'm pregnant.
Finally.
After all of these years, someone will love me forever.
I won't be too much.
They will think I am the most beautiful star they've ever seen.
David will stay.
He will love me more than he ever has before.
I'm making him a miracle.
You can't be possessed if you can make miracles, right?
The Virgin Mary, clean as snow.

Now,
me, too.

Second Trimester
I can hear the heartbeat of my baby girl.
She's going to be gorgeous; I know.
She will look like me.
And, I will tell her she is beautiful until she can't stand anymore.
There won't be any question that I love her.
She's going to know by the way I treat her.
I will be a good mother.
She will never feel the way my mother made me feel.
She won't be too much.

Third Trimester
I don't wanna tell my mom.
She's almost here.
My baby.
We've been homeless for a few months.
But, David's been right by my side
He thinks I am the most beautiful he's ever seen.
Since I've been pregnant,
I am afraid all this love,
all this excitement for me,
It will run out.

I don't want to disappear.
I wish Mama could see me.
I'm gonna be a mom.
A good mom.
My baby will love me
more than my own mama
loves me.

Birth
She's here.
And,
that's all they can see.
I am here, too.
I am never anyone's
everything.

Home
She cries all the time.
And, David or momma will come scoop her up.
Tell me to rest.
But, really, they don't care about me anymore.
It's all about that baby.
What a miracle I made.
(I hate her.)

Untitled (for now)

tender heart
soft
under belly
raw
unmet needs
left
to starve

To (M)other

Where does all the love you never gave me go?

Will it be buried in the grave
with you?

Past Self

Dear one,
I apologize for all the times
I judged you.

It was difficult to look at you
with compassion.
I acknowledge your bravery,
your innovation,
your thirst for more
than the present offered you

Thank you
for refusing table invitations where love
was not being served.

II.

blue

Primary
in its category:
**Why is blue
universal
for sorrow?**

What if
your sorrow
tastes more
like a mother
watching their child
fade away
of starvation?

Flavorless,
except
the salt
in tears.

or

What if it smells
of burned flesh
after found
sitting
in a bomb's way.

or

Is it felt like
the searing of skin
flashed by shrapnel
on your way to fill
your tin with food?

Is this blue
like sorrow
red like anger,

or,
maybe only
the whites of eyes
filled with greed?

Destabilized

It is a back
and forth.

The black waves
lap against the boat
if we keep moving.
But,
when we sit *still* in the black waters
the waves thrash.
The old wood of the vessel creaks.

I look to the storm-ladened sky
and then back to the dark waters.
They hold the shadows
of everything
that cannot be healed.

There is no white savior walking across these storm waters.
There is only *my* magic.
And
My magic doesn't wash it away with the tide.

It simply makes space
for the inevitable
for the possibilities
for the things
that resist treatment.

generated inheritance

i
wish my heart
was
large enough
to eat
the bloodied pain
you
passed on to me
as love

Mo(u)rning Dove

Your call beckons an inner darkness.
There is no staving away.
We must make lovers of the grief.

athame

I could not cut myself
d
e
e
p
enough
To bleed the grief all the way

                                      out.

holed

There are many wars being waged.
In every single moment
battles reveal
shrapnel laden riddles,
bullets lined like toothy grins.
We cannot begin to know.
We must only ever hold.

Hold

Hold

And pray to god that it's enough
for the levees that pack away
the grief
we fear to touch.

Shadow Holder

The Great Mother knows her Twins
She has memorized their faces
each any every dimple
and freckle
blemish

Even in the ashen storms
after air strikes
famine
all tenants of war
We must remember She will never forget the cries of horror

We pray she fills us
with the fortitude to endure
until the end.

Bear witness to your Earthen Family
Allow your heart to stay open
like the wound

knowing that it is the site
where **the light comes in**
and the shadow pours out

Why do we hold onto the earthbody?

Firmly
Relentlessly
Angrily

Why do we hold onto a body where we know life no longer resides?
Where rot will come home
eat its way out
and pass it to the rhizomes.
The soul is gone from this place.

"He is no longer here"

Why do we roll the stone away from a tomb
expecting a savior that was never ours?

lost guilt

The tepid, hard water rolls down my body.
Pores open to receive what pours out from above.
There are too many droplets to count.

The moments of guilt in my life,
they, like this water, come together
and form what feels like immovable borders,
places I cannot cross,
cracks in my imperfect view of self.

They say "*water remembers.*"
If this is true,
may it remember the times
 I knew who I was
before I allowed guilt to grow
like scaly bark
around my heart.

I close my eyes.
I pray to the water
asking it to forgive me
for all the times I said but didn't do
words spoken
that cut like dog teeth in flesh
glares that could turn Queen Medusa to stone
I am love, but have not always been loving.

My own waters erupt from morning-tired eyes.
They roll down cheeks and mix with earthwater
tying themselves together in fortification
for the baptism that is needed
to soften the hardened grief edges of my heart.

the lump in my throat

Not long ago:

Every time it began its resurrection
And,
made its rise,
I would swallow razors
made of lies
Disguised as protection.

"I need to"
Or
"There is no time to"
is what my mind framed
as the logical response.

Now:

As I write,
or bake,
rock my sick child,
re-member a wound,
I make welcome its rise,
as it gives way to
another version of me
that steps out of my shadow.

III.

The Breath I couldn't catch

"Congratulations!"
It's what they say
Like a script
But
It's laced with a layer of supremacy I am always encouraged never to forget
The place
They tried to carve for me
I am not your mule
Do not be surprised by my ability to rise
"Black imagination is
Sacred"[1]

Do you remember the night you fucked me to sleep?
Fever dream
Like the body before it breaks
Shivering
But hot
To the touch
Surges
Even my toes feel electric
Tongue
Mouth
Body dances
Convulsions
Peace

---

1 Quotation by Joy KMT

weeds

Sun beating down. Watered, fertilized. They keep cutting us down and we just grow back. They didn't know the struggle makes us more persistent. Freedom will come. Backs blown by the wind, bending. Sighing the songs of freedom.

Crushed

I didn't know that those who harmed me
did not actually possess the power to crush my spirit with words.
Why did I replay these lies, memorizing them as if they are sacred?

As if they belong

In my cells

Informing the Future of their worth

Instead of crushing
The hollowed bones
And painting my face
So that they might see themselves
And know their place

The Door

The Door

How many times have you reached for the handle and realized
Too late
That the handle was a portal
To a demon that did not recognize you as human
Instead
Your dark, brown eyes somehow morphed into razors that held machetes in their mouths
And gorillas for arms with serpents for teeth
(But, really you were just a young, brown Child with dreams of freedom between each tooth in a smile that illuminates ancestral answered prayers for survival)
You deserve better,
Young
Angel
Radiant
Life[2]

---

[2] Ralph Yarl, a 16 year old child at the time, was shot twice April 13, 2023 in Kansas City, MO for ringing the wrong doorbell while Black.

Muntu

I had a dream that they found the missing body of a Black man hacked up in a tree

I told them it was there but they didn't listen to me

You see, the trees, they whisper, if you listen. They are people, too.

So, they cut down the tree and found the pieces of Vaughn Miller. And, around each mutilated piece you could see how the tree had grown as if it tried to hold the mangled flesh in its arms, trying its best to bring the pieces together.

They cut down the tree, too.
Now, I have two funerals to attend[3]

---

[3] First published by Quenceira Press in 2023

Blood of the Land

They cannot imagine you as god.
You are too brown
Too wild
Wound, too deep.

Blood of the land
Braid your hair back into constellations.

The breadcrumbs will only be eaten by the buzzards.
And, we might lose our way.

The stars stay longer.
And,
It is easier to find yourself in the reflected fragments that light the sky
Than it is crawling on hand and knee[4]

---

[4] First published in *Kentucky Monthly*, February 2023

Black Femme

Black Femme,

Why do you cover your mouth when you laugh or cry?
Who taught you to mute your emotional experiences?

You are not a bridled animal

Unleash
Unfurl

Swallow those that try to eat you whole
Bones and all

Affirmations to the Black Woman

Black woman:
Friend.
Mother.
Sister.
There is
no groove
to get back.
You see
it was your bones
used
to carve
the way.
Your back
that carried
all.
Your blood
from which life
Springs.
Black woman:
There is no groove
deep enough
to contain you.

Black Kiing

Which one was it? Which death of a young brown boy taught my black brothers to walk the streets invisibly? Their eyes fall to the sidewalk like limp limbs, their bodies, tense. Was it Emmett? Tamir? Trayvon? Who told you that you were not born of royal blood? That the blood you carry pumps through a body upon which they still build kingdoms but refuse to let you enter? No, brown boy. Do not disappear on the sidewalk paved by hands that look like yours----powerful. Let them see you, kings.

I AM

A place of peace
Keeper of myself
Teller of my truth
Communal
AFROFUTURISM
Abundance
Water
Dynamic
Black Maverique
Full of voice
Embodied Joy
Worthy of Pleasure
I am
Playful
Transmutation, changing cellular DNA for generations to come
A portal for souls
Eloquent Rage
An experience
A nurturer
Boundlessly creative
Intuitive Seer
The sound on my skin
the oracle
the queerness
Creating spaces for new relationships not defined by the suppressive systems that have tried to choke out marginalized voices from being included in the stories of history.

IV.

When she reads

Her voice isn't a cliche
"like honey"
No, her voice is much more like an aged bourbon
going down like fire
and molasses.

And, that voice inches from my ear
into my chest
it burns
all the way down
and sweetens
as it sits warm
in my belly.

unto themselves

The heat hits the air
this deep, tepid and purplish night
It reminds me of the way
The condensation of your breath
dried on my Virgin skin
as you whispered that you could
"still taste" me
Hot shivers roll down and
meet the small of my back

Wetness collects
and that below skin
aching, throbbing of a heartbeat
Its drone drowns in the
dizzying dark of my mind

la petite mort de chocolat

Everything
is made better with
chocolate cake
made moist by mayonnaise
like somebody's granny
from Kentucky
stuck her toe in it
after casting the spell

Covered in a thick ass layer
of sugary, creamy icing
and sprinkled with
chocolate chips

Put it in the icebox for an hour
and
enjoy, naked, after
love making that leaves your legs
quivering
with a cup of coffee still steaming

Make sure the window is open
to catch the cool April breeze on your skin,
still damp
all this extends the orgasms
you howled
earlier by about an hour

You will never want to eat
chocolate cake
the same
ever
again.

An offered benefit of his "friendship"

Sweat like condensation
Hot house
Air thick like cotton
Wrap around porch

Legs, my legs
Stretched out

Arms, his arms
His voice, slow drawl poured into my ears
like honey in hot water
Sweet
His eyes, *unfocused*
bouncing from point to point on the ceiling
laughter like a melody that swings on the voice

It all
makes
me
weary.

Culmination

I apologize.

I have, my entire existence,
apologized for almost every single breath that entered my lungs.

There are so many deaths,
But
there have also been so many close encounters, too.
The stage on which I've been asked to play a role was designed to murder me.
So, when you say it's a culmination, know that I have also quietly wept, tears like salty moisturizer on the soft
hair of the sleeping child still nursing from my chest.
You were never alone in any of this.
I apologize.
It was never intentional to hold you hostage to all that I could never hold.

Compulsory Heterosexuality

It will not matter how many times
you try to choke out
The wound
The one
that reminds you
you were always too much
and
never
enough

No.

You will never scrub It out
no matter how many times
He kisses (those) lips

No.

That validation could never
make its home
within you

Not even
when he is in you
swaying
       groans
Grunts, "I love you"

No.

He never possessed the key
to that healing
but you will continue trying
any
way

Performance

No performance
of gender
will ever be
enough
for the idle gaze
of the wretched
moral binary

Shores

In the seam
that meets the water and earth
is
a third place
an existence
where duality meets its Death

When they as you
"What is their gender?"

tell them
it's in between the places
they cannot see

Where the heart
makes a mess
of the brain

sacral ache

That erotic
yearning
deep
inside
isn't for a lover;
it's you.

Love Letter to a little Non-Girl

Dear One.
You won't know your name yet
The colonizer's tongue thick in your throat
like cotton
It won't know what to call someone like you.
Some one
who knows what it means to be birthed
with your body
inside your soul
You will taste their fear of you
Do not swallow that pill
Instead
like Shiva
let it stay in your throat
alchemizing the poison
to speak medicine later
When you've learned how to speak
with your own voice
then, you will come to know your name
your soul whispers
every night

V.

1/5/2023 9:41p

As I take comfort in the smell of my sour, vinegared sweat caused by my medication to ward off the depression, I scroll mindlessly so I don't have to listen to the voices and fall back into the shadowed arms of sleep. Sometimes they are muffled, voiceless even. I feel their presence, always, but especially when I know they beckon me to play big like I love to say I do. There's a warm, achy throb in my chest. The spirit of the air shifts. I know they are here. There was a time I felt afraid of these ancestral knowings. This is because colonialism teaches us that these indigenous whisperings are only madness. I worked hard to turn the voices off. To mute the electrical noise. I received my diagnoses. Took my medication. And I tried to build the life expected of me. I was naive to think the smelling salts of Spirit would fall dull upon me. Or maybe beside me? But, certainly not *within* me. If I could still know them, would it mean the medication failed and I was a lost cause?

They say we are oracles. The queers. The ones who make questions out of the status quo. We hold the water full in the basins of our mouths for scrying. I am nervous, but not how you think. I am not nervous that I am crazy. My very existence as a descendant of slaves is madness. They didn't expect us to survive. I am a type of chaos. No, I am not afraid of being mad. I am afraid that in the standing stillness of listening and receiving that I will become more of my full self. I am afraid I will recognize my being as more than these embodied cells. There is danger in that recognition for them.

Ship(wrecked)

Blood Memories
are the anchor
If water remembers, what will my tears record today?

Re-*membering*
Marrow d e e p
"A charge to keep, I have…"

Death is an Artist
that sleeps beneath the sea I dug for it
when the salt-water from my earthen body
recorded the moment you drew back your love
recoiled with dark fingered hands
Now, the Artist calls for *my* sleep
but I am still yet entangled in those blood memories
that sink below, never to find an end

speaker, Wound

We, we get called on and that's the birth. Some of us grow as time passes. Others may die early. They call that a healing. Our bodies always leave a mark.

We are born and we are called to protect. To remind whoever carries us of where they may not go. We protect. We are safety. So, when the healings try to come and end us, like water, rising we must fight this dark baptism. I told you; we were born to protect. To remind the body of where they may never go if they wish to live.

Some of us, we come early. If you are born early, your chances of a long life increase drastically. When they are children, we can hold them close. Speak, and they will listen. They trust better when we meet them as children.

The work is hard. You must love the work to best shield the body from more danger. We live in the soft parts of the mind, the places where the whispers are loudest. They echo throughout the body, if you're lucky. If, you're good at your job. I'm surprised someone wants to know our story, my story. No one cares for a Wound to stay long, but we exist to save lives.

named yourself Witch

The stink of death drips
heavy in the stale air

The tuneful screams of the cicadas mark high summer
South
Count who's left after the hangings

I peel the slice of tangerine free
of its white ropes with my tongue
like a finished cord cutting ritual

I know it won't be long before they start
looking for my death body, too.
But
it won't be swinging from a tree.
I brought my own knife.

Divine, treasured

2 possum rib bones
an old flipping coin
pair of die

These were the things in the cherry wood jewelry box that Granny kept by her bed. Divination tools.
I walked around to the other side of the bed. It was made up, corners crisp. I sat down and dumped the items on the bed. I knew the purpose of the old, flipping coin. Yes or no questions. She'd brought it out a couple of times. The pair of die were off-white, the black paint worn on some of the inward half circles by encountering sweat and dirt. Each number had a meaning. But the possum bones. I didn't know their purpose exactly, well not in how they worked in divination. I do remember Granny telling me why she used them. She said our ancestors revered possums because they walked the hallowed grounds of the cemetery at night, keeping watch. **They are sacred animals.**

She was gone and yet she was in all these things. I felt I could still talk to her with these ordinary items some might even look at as trash. She'd kept them like they were treasures, though, in that antique jewelry box.

Marked

Marked by a number
bowing heads sing their hunger
waiting for yellowed illumination
like the sun pouring its rays in
just below dawn

Which portal will you dream to life?

Bird feet, dances
make marks in dried dust
The harvest came too soon
and the elm trees wept.

Why didn't they tell us when we were children that when we die, we don't become angels?

Why didn't they tell us when we were children that when we die, we don't become angels?

We sit in dark trees with crow eyes for feet waiting for the next call to a fleshly domain
Paint the ceiling of the wrap around porch blue so they know they can't stay here

The whispering shadows on the walls play breathless games of ring around roses triggering the ringing in your ears

Shadows that remind you that you're never alone and heaven was only created so that you'd work harder for the monsters stuffed in zombied skin that live down the lane.
The monsters that don't give a damn if you live or die so long as there's another body waiting in line to fill your place.

I'd rather stay a crow eye whisper, making rooms in haint spaces

Heretic

Wide, gaped mouth
chewing the air violently
choking on dry communion
but no sound escapes the throat
or at least none
I can hear

There was a time
when the voice of the oppressor was so loud
I confused it with my own
but my un-baptism in the dark waters
of my soul
killed the monster

Acid melting its skin off bone until
It was lily white
now I use them to divine

No, the unholy mess of man-made trauma
can now leave on the boat
that took my ancestors
from their home.

The Caul

It sounded like the scream of my father
And yet, my gut wrenched
as if it had spilled forth from my own soul
Paralyzed
Was it real?
Or
My brain
Is it sick again?
Staring blankly in the dark my mind turns pages to find the source
Stolen bodies on stolen land…
Perhaps it was my father from years ago
wailing loss
The sound of broken bone
Black-green waters, sea
They wash up on the shore
bloated
and freed
I've been free this whole time
baptized now by spiritual waters, sea
of ancestral bonds
unbroken
unlike the bones of my father that night

care

"Who made the pound cake?"
Is what she asked me
While dinner cooled on the stove
I had been trying to tell her
I don't go to school anymore
but the air from my breath kept getting trapped in my hallowed throat

"Is it gluten-free?"
I hold her lies each year
that beneath the tree
the skull is hidden
black from bruise blue

The ax fell upon the knife
The anger swept up the wind
from the impending storm

She never told Venus
"I loved him better."
Now, the evergreen grass grows
over the corpses of
their hidden love
"I can't tell the heat is on. My feet are cold."

In Remembrance

When I remember, I re-member

the many ghosts
of me
that died
in
utero

arm
    foot
finger

now one large conglomeration

sliver of nail
yellowed tooth
the working root spoke
in hallowed drawl
an ever-present memory
of a tongue forced in mouth
after mother muscle cut out

faint smell of metal
tasting ripe air

the heat
never like home
always plantation house

How far generated does learned trauma reach forth to pull back?

VI.

The Fool

Our entrance into this realm of existence
is one of bursts of light and pain
Before the journey
there is a great forgetting
we come back again
again
again
Shouldered on each side of the portal,
the (M)other Wound
the last few visions of the Mission
but they flash by too quickly
to be imprinted

Soul Met Body Met Soul

You were born embodied
Body in soul
Soul not new
Newness comprised of cells
Cells cannot keep you
You are bigger than the box
Boxed and shelved with dust
Dust that settled into cracks in skin
Skins of heaven
Heaven in Earth
Earth in You.

attachment

security
it is not held in ~~sameness~~
it is not perfection
it is not the absence of pain

it is the active pursuit of
repair

time
again and
again
again, weaving
vulnerability
through and
out
the ear
to **heart**

sensing

we say
we are blind in the dark
that all is lost
that nothing may be seen

but
this is not the complete truth
is seeing only done
with eyes?

do you not have
other senses
that might lead you
to the light
that resides
within?

Einalia

I can let her carry my body

Breathless

Out to the deepest ending
salt water bloated
So I might finally be
swollen enough
to hold the grief
Will my body burn
when it reaches the edge?

Where the water
meets the Sun

holy

When I was young

looking at my dark brown skin
illuminated underneath the colored stained glass
I memorized that I was holy

but
only under certain terms

under certain bodies
under the thick, oxblood leather of the Book
I memorized that my access to sacredness

must be bleached washed in lily of the valley white

holiness achieved only by the swallowing

of stale bread
grape juice
and
the loss of any and all of what might make me

me
desire

lust
red-handed

queerness
these exist on a larger list that,

for a while
I could not name

or utter

without feeling the deepest shame
The reclamation of the mind is a dangerous thing
But,
the question is

who is in danger?

Me

or

the institution that asked me to abandon myself
for a white man who didn't exist to save me
or my ancestors?
If I reclaim my mind and recover my power,

how many hail Marys must I say to pull the hood from *her* son's face?

soiled

I am not afraid to make dirty my hands
(*however*)
Your hands will never be clean of me

Venus in Leo

Fire golds
run deep
in blood reds

take on the sun
weave its essence into your sinews
so that the fibers underneath skin
might glow
and burn away
your doubt
of your own divinity

if you would only allow yourself
to ingest your own magnificence
allow it to poison the deep well

full of the questions
that keep their lies etched in the muscles of your heart

Strawberry Moon

It's almost time for the screaming
They lie dormant in the ground

Sleeping

When the time comes
they emerge in triumph
to wail in the trees
and *fuck*

How sweet and simple the delicious life of a cicada must be
bursting through all at once into the sticky heat of high summer

Home of sun tea
shucked beans
and ripening green tomatoes on a chipped window sill
flung open to catch the wet thickness of an Alabama summer breeze

Can you hear the screaming?
It's almost time.

(un)write

As I write myself into existence
(finally alive, no longer alien)
I unwrite the lies I swallowed and did my best to embody as truth
(finally alive, no longer alien)

I unwrite
- a misunderstanding of sexuality: I am allowed to be desirous, hungry, even unquenchable

I unwrite
- the lie that we must stand in either/or: I am both, I am neither. I am everything all at once, a contradiction

I unwrite
- that my skin is too dark, freckled like a ripe strawberry: I will never rub it away

I unwrite
- the limitations of my Blackness: Everything I touch is Black, like Midas but make it

Hoodoo

As I write myself into existence
I realize the truth
I *re* member the ancient dreams

I stitch together stars,
and collect the gasses of Jupiter and Neptune
to compose a body unbridled by fear.

I unwrite to *rewrite.*

Silas wisdom

She sits on my lap
singing some song with made-up words
gobble garbled sounds
there is so much joy in her musicking

I think:

Once I was just like this
full of my entire self
and
I don't want this to end for her

the engulfed, embodied self-love
I want her to stay grounded in these moments of exquisite mundanity

She's fallen asleep
worn down by hours of play and exploration
Why do we exchange this for the enslavement of adulthood?
I will fall asleep, too

but, from exhaustion of masking
my play pretend is a melancholic ostinato
that hums underneath the weariest smile

Samuel wisdom

He dreams thousands of years
and they connect to the center
he told me once he went *through*
through the center of the earth
and on the other side
he met himself
and others
from thousands of years

dark hair
coarse
dark eyes
wisdom heavy
dark skin
ancient embodied

they spoke in a language he said he only
re-members in his dreams

upon waking
he asks to tend to the altar
to give thanks to the ones before
who are here now
and walk before us

splitting time
so that we
might take histories
and make them our own

altar

she grabs a fistful
of innocence
clovers
flowers and all
offers them up
dusting the ripped greens
from chubby fingers
onto a covered bookcase

they will dry
in death

then I will brush them
into my hand
worn well from
the work
mindful to catch
each piece
smile
and throw them
away

Our Breath is Revolutionary

There were ten today
ten who came and sat their roots down
bloody and dusty from a fresh pull from their Beings

and they wrote
what is
what was
and
what shall always **be**

in the circle they placed their roots at the center
some not knowing the magic within
the healing that could take place once consumed
but everyone
took

There was *enough*

In incantations, low voiced
cackles bright like lightening flashes
they spoke
shaking the earth to its own rock molten soul

She said the Sun is Black
while another told of our sacred bodies being filled to the brim with
unspeakable art
they howled like a slow burning ache
a remembrance offering
ancestral in nature

Taking needles, they wove promises of their future work
into the quilt of sky
hanging high beneath them

they made oaths to themselves that they would be first
no longer last
(*or not at all*)

After the circle was complete,
their sacred smiles creeping at mouth corners,
They walked away
but never from each other

—For the womxn in the BIPOC Writing What Is circle that changed my life

ungendering

It isn't that simple, the *ungendering*. It is not an article of clothing I choose to put on or pull off. Do you know what it's like to wake up in a body that confuses the idle gazes that follow you? I am not as I seem. I cannot be discovered or understood in your glance. **My body** tells *my story*. Most come with their own in mind. It feels impossible to them to believe any experience outside their own. It cannot be…seeing is believing and the script has been written. It is so lonely here. Isolation swallows you whole when you cannot be the expectation: the version they designed for you…*of you.*

Some say we are oracles, portals,
pools of darkened water that catch the reflections of refracted light.
we give things names. But does the thing know' itself by that name?
Does the warmth of the sun know it's varying degrees?
or is it only itself, stretching, blanketing, providing food.
it is only as it knows itself.
I have been named many
times in efforts to keep me contained,
to know me.
          But what do you call an experience **EMBODIED**?

The answers to what experience I am are not written upon this flesh. This fleshy mold that houses my soul will never tell you who or what I am. Knowing requires listening and believing whatever you have been told as true. There is never a moment you know any *body* to tell you every **soul**. We are so much more than whatever we dream up: to try and hold the understanding that spills over our cupped hands and rushes down, bleeding to touch whatever stands in the path.

Samar Jade (they/them) is a Black, fat, disabled and gender expansive creative writer and Ensoulment Doula. Samar's writing centers the experiences of being born and raised in the Deep Gothic South. Their poetry has been published by *Pile Press, Kentucky Monthly,* and *Quenceria Press* and their fiction short story "Ghosts" will be published in a collection with Roots, Wounds, Words. *Blue Violet: Haint Spaces* is their debut full length poetry collection. When Smar isn't writing or ferrying others in their underworld journeys, they enjoy spending time with their partner and two children.

www.ingramcontent.com/pod-product-compliance
Lightning Source LLC
Chambersburg PA
CBHW030057170426
43197CB00010B/1556